Missing

True Cases of Mysterious Disappearances 2

Andrew J. Clark

All rights reserved © 2020 by Andrew J. Clark. No part of this publication or the information in it may be quoted from or reproduced in any form by means such as printing, scanning, photocopying, or otherwise without prior written permission of the copyright holder.

Effort has been made to ensure that the information in this book is accurate and complete. However, the author and the publisher do not warrant the accuracy of the information, text, and graphics contained within the book due to the rapidly changing nature of science, research, known and unknown facts, and internet. The author and the publisher do not hold any responsibility for errors, omissions, or contrary interpretation of the subject matter herein. This book is presented solely for motivational and informational purposes only.

ISBN: 9798664028188

Printed in the United States

Contents

Where Did They Go?	1
Did Jim Sullivan Hitch a Ride on a UFO?	3
The Last Patrol of Alan Addis	11
Hunrath and Wilkinson Snatched by the Space Brothers	17
What Happened to Maura Murray?	21
The Last Known Whereabouts of Tara Calico	27
Diane Augat	33
Where's She At?	33
Ciara Breen	39
Where Have You Been?	39
Asha Degree	45
Vanished off the Face of the Earth	45
Looking for Mathew Greene	49
Where's Jennifer Dulos?	53
Oscar Zeta Acosta	57
The Brown Buffalo and his Boat of White Snow	57
Gary Mathias and the Yuba Five	61
The Tragic Case of Diane Suzuki	67
In Search of Amy Bechtel	73
How Elijah Disappeared in the Blink of an Eye	79
Finding Them	83
Further Readings	85

Where Did They Go?

Every single year, thousands of people go missing. Most of these missing person cases are eventually solved, but there are a stubborn few that continue to defy explanation. There are cases in which folks seem to disappear into thin air with no sign or trace of where they may have gone.

In the case of Jim Sullivan, for example, a struggling yet promising musician vanished while heading to Nashville. The guy's first album, named *U.F.O.*, has since become a cult classic even while the cause of Jim's disappearance remains a mystery. The album's title has predictably given rise to jokes that Jim met up with one of the UFOs he sang about, but in reality, no one has a clue what may have happened to the man.

Another case described in this book, that of the so-called Yuba Five, presents an equally perplexing mystery in which four men inexplicably perished in the wilderness while a fifth was never seen again. One of the victims died of starvation and hypothermia—in a warm cabin stocked with food. Such cases leave investigators—and the rest of us—absolutely baffled.

Other mysterious disappearances take on a much more sinister hue, with clear indications of foul play—yet with no body forthcoming, they remain listed as missing person cases. Both Diane Suzuki's disappearance in the 1980s and the much more recent disappearance of Jennifer Dulos fit this category. It seems likely that both women were murdered, but in the absence of their remains, all we can really say is that they are missing.

It could very well be that many of the vanished ran into some sort of foul play along the way—but even so, many of the cases provide so few clues that one can only wonder and speculate as to what may have transpired. And all of the stories presented here in this book will leave you truly scratching your head as you ask yourself, "Where did they go?"

Did Jim Sullivan Hitch a Ride on a UFO?

Who: Jim Sullivan
When: March 6, 1975
Where: New Mexico

Context

Jim Sullivan was a promising yet troubled musician who disappeared in search of the ultimate dream. He had dropped an exciting and well-produced rock/folk album called *U.F.O.* in 1969, but became disillusioned when it failed to chart. He was still struggling to get his musical career off the ground in 1975 when he announced to his friends and family that he was going to make the trek from Los Angeles to Nashville in search of the fame and stardom that had thus far eluded him.

But somewhere on that journey, Jim Sullivan disappeared without a trace. To this very day, no one knows exactly what happened to this forlorn folk singer, and all we have to remember him by is an obscure masterwork called *U.F.O.* This album, full of enchanting lyrics describing far-off vistas and strange visitations, must stand as Jim's final testament.

Jim grew up in San Diego, California, where he enjoyed football as much as music and played quarterback in high school. After hearing some local blues bands, he got a guitar and started playing the blues, and soon he started his own band—the Survivors—and began to write his own rock, folk and blues tunes.

Meanwhile, he married a woman named Barbara and had a son with her. This young family then moved to Los Angeles, where Jim—like many musicians before and since—hoped to make it big. Barbara became the breadwinner, working long hours at Capital Records, while Jim stayed home perfecting his music.

And although Jim wasn't bringing home the bacon, he seemed to be doing something right. He was becoming increasingly well-known at the bars where he played gigs, and even Hollywood celebrities such as Lee Majors, Harry Dean Stanton and Lee Marvin had taken note of him. But the acclaim was all local, and no matter how many clubs Jim played in, he just couldn't seem to break through to the next level and secure a record deal.

Following a series of rejections by Capitol Records, Jim was feeling frustrated when he lucked out and met a small-time music producer named Al Dobbs while performing at a local joint called The Raft. Al liked what he heard and agreed to release Jim's first album on his own label, Monnie. *U.F.O.* came out in 1969, and with Jim's original vocals backed up by seasoned session musicians, many who heard it considered it nothing short of a masterpiece.

Yet as any veteran of the music world could attest, breaking out into superstardom is not just a matter of how good you are but a matter of how lucky you get. There are plenty of guitarists, vocalists, and even whole bands of rock-solid musicians as good as anyone you hear on the radio who never make the playlist. Jim Sullivan released his album and waited for that lucky break—and waited, and waited.

In the meantime, he kept hobnobbing with the stars, but that didn't get him much other than a part as an extra in the quintessential youth rebellion flick *Easy Rider*. One track from *U.F.O.*, "Rosey", was released as a single in 1970 but attracted relatively little interest.

Disappointed but undaunted, Jim managed to get another record deal in 1972, this time with Playboy Records. Yes, *that* Playboy—Hugh Hefner had momentarily taken his eyes off his centerfolds to dabble in the record business. The problem was, that sounded just as funny back in the early 70s as it does today. Playboy was never taken seriously as a music label, and the records it released were seen more as novelties than anything else. Thus it was unsurprising that Jim's self-titled sophomore album fared even worse than *U.F.O.* Depressed and despairing over his inability to succeed in the music business, Jim began to drink heavily, and the strain was soon evident in his family life. By 1975 Jim was despondent and desperate to change his losing hand. He decided to make one last mad dash for fame and head for Nashville, Tennessee, hoping that the country music capital might give him the opening that Los Angeles and Hollywood had not. He left California on March 4, 1975, telling his family and friends that he would return shortly—but they would never see him again.

On That Day

The next day Barbara received an enigmatic phone call from her husband. The first thing he said was that he was alright, but when she asked where he was and what he was doing, Jim replied, "You wouldn't believe [me] if I told you." Barbara invited him to try telling her anyway, but Jim just cut her off: "Forget it. Just forget I said anything. I'll call you from Nashville."

As it turned out, nothing very mysterious had happened to Jim at this point. He'd been pulled over on a highway in New Mexico on (almost certainly justified) suspicion of drunk driving but had been let go with a warning. Shortly thereafter he checked into La Mesa Motel in Santa Rosa. But if the cop had ordered Jim to go sleep off the booze, he wasn't about to comply. Right after checking in and calling Barbara, he went to a local liquor store to load up on vodka. The next time he was spotted he was about 26 miles farther east, walking along Route 66 near a ranch owned by the Gennitti family.

Jim's abandoned car was found several days later, complete with all of his documents, clothes, and money. He had also left behind a box of his records and his guitar. Seeing as how his main purpose in going to Nashville was to play music and promote himself, that was not a good sign, to say the least.

Investigation

What happened to Jim Sullivan? Since he was never again seen alive, it's easy to assume that he met his bitter end in the New Mexico desert. Then again, his body had never been found, either. Sure enough, *a* body was found near the Gennitti ranch during the search following his disappearance—but it wasn't Jim's, and as there was no indication that it had anything to do with him, the mystery only continued.

Some speculated that this frustrated musician, unable to accept that he had not achieved the stardom he craved, committed suicide by wandering into the desert. Many of his friends, however, insisted that despite his depression, Jim wasn't suicidal. And that opens up another possibility. What if Jim didn't die in that desert—but his dreams of making the *Billboard* charts did? Could it be that he literally walked away from it all and shed his old life for a new one, under a new identity, somewhere else?

As far-fetched as such a thing may seem, it does happen sometimes. In 1993, for example, a man named Richard Hoagland (not to be confused with former NASA consultant and conspiracy theorist Richard C. Hoagland) abandoned his family in Indiana and disappeared without a trace. He too might have made the pages of this book had it not come to light in 2016 that he'd fled to Florida and stolen a dead man's identity to elude anyone who was trying to find him.

Richard Hoagland wanted a new life, and he took a very drastic step to get one. Could Jim Sullivan have done the same thing? Is he living somewhere else under an assumed name and identity, far from his past heartaches and disappointments?

Well, Barbara used to say that perhaps Jim was abducted by the UFO "he'd written about in his songs." It's unclear how serious she was, but in the utter absence of any evidence to the contrary, that hypothesis seems just about as good as any!

Update

In 2010, a man who just happened to be named Matt Sullivan came across Jim Sullivan's old *U.F.O.* album and fell in love with both the music and the story behind it. So much so that he re-released *U.F.O.* on his Light in the Attic label—and also kicked off a new inquest into what happened to Jim.

Matt conducted a number of interviews with Jim's friends, family, and associates, but these efforts yielded very little new information. It wasn't a complete loss, though, because while Matt was knee-deep in Jim's life, he managed to dig up a real diamond from the ashes and put together a compilation of unreleased Jim Sullivan tracks. The new album was issued in 2019 as *If the Evening Were Dawn*.

The Last Patrol of Alan Addis

Who: Alan Addis
When: August 8, 1980
Where: Falkland Islands

Context

Alan Addis was born in 1961 and joined the Royal Marines while he was still in his teens. He was posted to the far-off Falkland Islands, located off Argentina east of the southern tip of South America. The United Kingdom had controlled the territory for hundreds of years, but by the latter half of the 20th century, Argentina was becoming increasingly covetous. This tension would soon erupt in the Falklands War when Argentine forces invaded the islands in 1982—but Alan Addis wouldn't be there to witness the conflict, because he vanished without a trace in August of 1980.

On That Day

The 19-year-old Alan served in Naval Party 8901, which was in the Falklands as a "strategic tripwire" in case Argentina attempted to seize the islands. The Marines were also tasked with preparing the largely British population to resist Argentine aggression, and they had managed to pull together some 120 civilian volunteers to shore up the islands' defenses. Alan and his comrades had thus gotten to know the locals fairly well, and on the evening of August 8th, a small group of them attended a gathering at the village hall in the settlement of North Arm (which despite the name is actually located on the southern end of East Falkland). Alan was last seen at the hall sometime after 1:30 AM.

The next morning, his brothers in arms boarded a boat back to the Falkland capital of Stanley. Only after the boat left North Arm did they realize that Alan Addis was missing. Some speculated that he'd gone AWOL after meeting some friendly local girl at the village hall; others worried that he'd fallen overboard. As the days progressed with no sign of him, many more questions would arise.

Investigation

A massive investigation was launched shortly after Alan's disappearance. Reconnaissance boats and aircraft methodically combed the surrounding area but found no sign of his body. Investigators were stumped, but Alan's mother, Anne, was not willing to give up on her son so easily. In the fall of 1981, she headed to the Falklands to personally oversee the search for the missing soldier.

Anne soon came to believe that her son's disappearance was no accident. Someone was behind it—she just didn't know who, or why. As her suspicions grew, she requested for the Ministry of Defence to open an inquiry into what had happened. The inquiry was duly conducted by the Special Investigations Branch (SIB) of the Royal Military Police. But even though it was Anne who initiated this investigation, she wouldn't be privy to the results. In the end, the SIB officer in charge tagged his report CONFIDENTIAL, and Anne wasn't able to read one word of it.

Anne's quest for the truth suffered another setback when the Falklands War broke out and precious files collected during the investigation went missing. She continued keeping her ear to the ground, however, and in 1993 she received word of a rumor that a Falklander had recently bragged about being involved in Alan's death.

This was certainly not what any mother would want to hear, but it was what Anne had long suspected, and if it brought her any closer to closure, she was going to pursue this grim clue for all it was worth. She forwarded her new bit of information to the Royal Falkland Islands Police, and it became part of a larger re-opening of the case and a renewed search for answers.

A new team of investigators quickly dispelled some of the more baseless rumors, but they did determine that Alan Addis was most likely murdered by locals. They even zeroed in on four persons of interest and arrested all four of them—before reaching yet another dead end and releasing them.

The next major development occurred in 1997 when a team of forensic archaeologists from the University of Birmingham set out to see if they could locate Alan's remains. The group made expert use of ground-penetrating radar and a cadaver dog to look through numerous locations where it was hypothesized that Alan might be—but the search turned up absolutely nothing.

This result might be seen as heartening since it left open the possibility that Alan was still alive, but it did nothing to close the case or provide closure to Alan's mother. Anne doggedly kept up her investigation, and in December of 2010, she received a tip from a Falklands resident who claimed to know where Alan was buried. The Metropolitan Police promptly headed to the islands to investigate and conduct yet another search, but once again they came back empty handed.

Update

Sadly, Anne Addis passed away in 2011 with her son's disappearance still unresolved. Others, however, have taken up the search for Alan in her honor. In the summer of 2018, the British Forces Broadcasting Service posted on YouTube a special documentary on the disappearance. The documentary brought forward more Falklanders who were present around the time of Alan's disappearance, and they theorized that he might have been killed "in a fight over a woman."

Such conflicts between locals and British troops were relatively common back then. Was Alan murdered in a fit of jealous rage? There's still a lot more to this case that needs to be sorted out, but hopefully, the renewed interest will bring about a better understanding of what actually happened to Alan Addis in the Falkland Islands all of those years ago.

Hunrath and Wilkinson Snatched by the Space Brothers

Who: Karl Hunrath & Wilbur Wilkinson
When: November 10, 1953
Where: California

Context

Karl Hunrath and Wilbur Wilkinson—electrical engineers by trade—disappeared without a trace after developing an avid interest in UFOs. Just one sentence into this story and it certainly *sounds* strange—and oh yes, it is!

In January of 1952, Karl believed, he had come into contact with an alien intelligence. He was asleep in his bed when he woke up to find a tall, skinny figure standing over him. The figure looked human enough, with one head, two arms, and two legs. It even wore what looked like a bespoke suit. But after it jabbed a needle into Karl's arm, giving him a dose of some kind of drug that made him feel "spaced out," it assured him that it was not of this Earth: "I am Bosco. You have been chosen to enter our brotherhood of galaxies."

Despite that, Karl couldn't help but feel that the being had a European accent. Nevertheless, he sat back and listened politely as the intruder informed him that he was "special" and had been "chosen to help the aliens prevent" the "end of the world." Bosco then "flooded" Karl with all kinds of "technical and science-based imagery" which seemed to be downloaded right into his brain before leaving the room through an open window.

Shortly after this alleged visitation, Karl got his pal Wilbur Wilkinson to follow him out west so they could be close to the burgeoning community of UFO enthusiasts in California. This was the land of George Adamski and the so-called "contactees" who claimed to be in regular contact with extraterrestrials, and Karl and Wilbur got to know Adamski pretty well. On one occasion, they were even kicked off his property after Karl started ranting and raving about how Bosco had told him that the aliens could easily destroy the U.S. Air Force.

Adamski told Karl and company to take a hike because he suspected that the walls had ears— and while his views on UFOs have yet to be proven, that's one thing he was definitely right about. The FBI was indeed monitoring him, and shortly thereafter agents showed up to ask about Karl and Wilbur. A panicked Adamski was quick to wash his hands of the pair, but perhaps he needn't have. Karl and Wilbur were not going to be bothering Adamski—or anyone else—much longer.

On That Day

On November 10, 1953, Karl and his buddy drove a rental car to a private airstrip. Karl was a seasoned pilot and had arranged to rent a small airplane, telling the agency that he was flying out to meet some "friends" in the desert. What he told Wilbur was a little bit different: He said they were flying out to the middle of nowhere to meet up with a UFO. Wilbur apparently leaped at the prospect of meeting the ETs that Karl claimed to be in contact with.

The trip was supposed to be a brief one, so when late afternoon arrived without a word from their clients or a glimpse of their plane, the folks at the flight agency started to get nervous. Another party who was quite concerned was Wilbur's wife, who was well aware of her husband and his buddy Karl's odd interest in UFOs. She knew that Wilbur would follow Karl just about anywhere—but she never imagined that he would fly into the desert and never return. As the only person who really knew what was going on with the pair, it was Mrs. Wilkinson who filled the press in on all of the strange details regarding her husband Wilbur and his friend Karl Hunrath.

Investigation

In the following weeks, an exhaustive search was conducted in the United States, as well as in Mexico and Canada, but no sign of the men or the plane they flew out on was ever found. No one knows what happened, but speculation continues to run rampant. Perhaps it was Wilbur's widow (?) who summed it up best: "I just can't help but think that flying saucers really had something to do with their disappearance."

Update

This mysterious disappearance has been speculated about for several decades, but there are still no leads and no new updates. Karl Hunrath and Wilbur Wilkinson have yet to be found.

What Happened to Maura Murray?

Who: Maura Murray
When: February 9, 2004
Where: Vermont

Context

Maura Murray, a 21-year-old student at the University of Massachusetts, disappeared in 2004 and hasn't been seen since. The first sign that something was amiss came on the evening of February 9th, when a passerby called the police to report that a car had slid off the road and was submerged in the falling snow.

On That Day

It was a cold and wintery day in the Northeast and the roads were slick, so the caller's report was hardly surprising. But when police came to investigate, they found the car completely abandoned. They ran the plates and found that it belonged to Maura Murray, but they had no idea where she was. Presumably, she had lost control on the ice and snow, but if so, what happened after that? She could have left the car and headed out on foot to get help, but it didn't seem that she could have gotten far. Had she somehow met her end walking along the cold and icy road?

Later that evening, police received their first lead. A bus driver named Buch Atwood claimed that he had come across Maura after the crash and found her to be "cold, but unharmed." He offered to get help for her, but she "begged him not to call the police." Nevertheless, as soon as Atwood got home, which was just a little way away, he called the police—who by this point had a very good idea why the young woman didn't want them to be involved.

Investigation

Investigators had found several open containers of alcohol in the abandoned car, indicating that Maura was most likely drunk when she crashed her car. She herself, though, was still nowhere to be found. When the police contacted her worried family, they were just as bewildered as anyone else as to where she could have gone. Her father, Fred, reported that she'd been fine when he'd seen her the day before—although it turned out that Maura's own car wasn't the first one she'd run off the road in the last couple of days.

Fred had lent her his Toyota Corolla the day before that because she wanted to drive to a campus party. Now, giving your car to a 21-year-old bound to a college keg party might not sound like such a great idea—and it wasn't. On the way back from the party, Maura crashed the car into a guardrail. But she wasn't injured, and the easy-going Fred wasn't upset. When she told him about the accident, he shrugged it off and told her not to worry about it. The car was fully insured, he said, and the insurance company would pay to have it fixed. Fred thought that was the end of the story.

Maura, though, was busy making up a story of her own. The next day—on that fateful February 9th—she fired off several emails to her teachers and the manager at her job, informing them that there had been a "death in the family" and she would be taking a week off. Fred told investigators that no one had died—and he had no idea why Maura would have made up such a story to get a week off.

Shortly after sending the emails, Maura drove to a nearby ATM and took out 280 bucks. Straight after that, she hit up the local liquor store and spent about 40 dollars on vodka and other hard liquor. She seemed like a girl on a mission, but no one was sure exactly what that mission was.

The police did find one clue, however. Inside her car were printed MapQuest directions (doesn't that bring you back to the early 2000s!) to a luxury condo in Burlington, Vermont. And a quick look at Maura's phone records showed that she had called someone at this location before she disappeared. Yet no other leads in this direction were forthcoming.

Upon examining Maura's dorm room, investigators found her stuff packed and the room "neatly cleaned." But most unsettling was a printed email she had left on top of one of the neatly stacked boxes. This email detailed problems with her boyfriend, Bill Rausch, and seemed to indicate that a breakup was on her mind.

In later years, several people claimed to have spotted a girl matching Maura's description around Burlington, but besides these alleged sightings, there have been no further clues to her whereabouts. For all intents and purposes, she simply disappeared.

Update

One of the chief investigators in Maura's case, James Renner, has long held to the theory that she simply ran off to start a new life. He was so certain of this, in fact, that in October of 2018 he issued a public statement that if Maura Murray were in fact still alive and wishing to be left alone, all he needed was private confirmation of this fact and he would cease his investigation.

Strangely enough, it was just a few months later, on December 31st of that year, that Renner suddenly took down his blog detailing the search for Maura Murray. Did Maura indeed contact him and ask him to back off? Renner hasn't said, so it's just speculation—but it's also quite a coincidence!

The Last Known Whereabouts of Tara Calico

Who: Tara Calico
When: September 20, 1988
Where: New Mexico

Context

The disappearance of Tara Calico presents a complete mystery. Investigators have tried to get a lead on this strange case for many years, but have only found themselves at a dead end.

On That Day

Tara Calico was last seen on September 20, 1988, when she headed out on her bicycle with her Sony Walkman and a tape of the rock band Boston in hand. As usual, her route took her along New Mexico's busy State Road 47. A number of people would later recall seeing the happy-go-lucky girl cruising past on her bike jamming to her tunes, but none of them saw anything untoward happening. The only possible inkling that she might have met with foul play was a report of a pickup truck that at one point seemed to be "following closely behind her." But something must have happened somewhere along the way because Tara Calico never returned home from that fateful bike ride.

Investigation

Tara had asked her mother, Patty, to drive her to her boyfriend's house for a planned game of tennis later that afternoon. When Tara wasn't back by lunchtime, Patty went out and cruised along her daughter's favorite bike route, worried that she might have had a flat tire, or God forbid, an accident. When she couldn't find any sign of Tara, she got a lot more worried and called the police.

The cops immediately converged on the scene and retraced Tara's steps. They didn't find her, but what they did find left an ominous impression: a trail of broken pieces of plastic that were all that was left of Tara's prized Sony Walkman and Boston cassette tape. Unfortunately, this debris didn't lead them anywhere, and the case went cold until the following year.

On June 15, 1989, a Polaroid picture was found discarded in a convenience store parking lot in Port St. Joe, Florida. The photo came to the attention of law enforcement because of its startling subject matter. It showed a young woman and a boy sitting bound and gagged on a bed, with their hands tied behind their backs and duct tape covering their mouths. The woman was dressed in a T-shirt and shorts—and she looked a lot like Tara.

The woman who found the photo didn't know that, of course, but she knew that something was very wrong with the picture. As soon as she picked it up from where a "white windowless Toyota cargo van" had been sitting just moments before, she walked over to the convenience store's payphone and called the police. She told them that the driver of the van was a man with a mustache who appeared to be in his 30s. The police immediately set up multiple roadblocks in the area, but they had no luck in finding the vehicle. All they could do then was forward the photo to national law enforcement agencies to see if anyone, anywhere, could identify the woman and boy it depicted.

When the photo was eventually shown to Patty, she asserted that—minus the makeup that she usually wore—the girl resembled her daughter. She also noticed that the girl in the photo seemed to have a scar on her leg just like the one Tara had. This prompted experts at Los Alamos National Laboratory to perform an in-depth comparison to determine whether it was really Tara in the Polaroid, but the results were inconclusive.

One thing that was learned was that the photo couldn't have been taken until May of 1989 since the particular type of Polaroid film used was not available until then. That was a full eight months after Tara's disappearance, and investigators were divided as to what that meant. Some saw it as a hopeful sign that Tara was still alive. Others reasoned that a kidnapper would have been unlikely to keep her alive for that long and that the woman in the photo probably wasn't Tara after all.

Update

In 2008, the case took a new and unexpected turn. The Sheriff of Valencia County, Rene Rivera, received a tip that Tara had been the victim of a hit and run accident that had been covered up. Remember the tailgating pickup truck noted by witnesses to Tara's last bike ride? Well, the tipster claimed that this truck had accidentally struck the girl and then the panicked driver and passenger had covered it up by disposing of her corpse and keeping the whole thing quiet for 20 years.

If this is what actually happened, it would explain a lot. If Tara was hit by a truck, her Walkman could well have been smashed as well or at least knocked into the road to be run over by other vehicles. Patty had previously theorized that Tara purposefully broke the device while she was being kidnapped to leave a trail of evidence, like so many Sony breadcrumbs, for investigators to follow. But the fact is, most of us would not think to do something like that when cornered by an abductor. By contrast, the idea that the Walkman was smashed in a car accident appears much more plausible.

But even with this tantalizing new lead from an anonymous tipster, without a body, and without any further evidence to corroborate this decidedly different version of events, the case still remains unresolved.

Diane Augat
Where's She At?

Who: Diane Augat
When: April 10, 1998
Where: Odessa, Florida

Context

Of all the mysterious disappearances so far discussed in this book, Diane Augat is probably the most troubling. Diane was born in 1958 and grew up in a loving family. She then seemed perfectly poised to start her own solid family unit, with a loving husband and children to boot. But by 1988, her mental health had begun to unravel and she was diagnosed with bipolar disorder. As her mental world came unglued, her marriage fell apart and she lost custody of her children. After her divorce, she went to live with family, but her relatives found her increasingly hard to control and she began bouncing back and forth between their homes and various mental institutions. Just prior to her disappearance, Diane Augat was living with her sister Deborah Cronin in Odessa, Florida.

On That Day

Diane stepped out of her family's lives for good on April 10, 1998. On that fateful day, Deborah had left the house for a medical appointment, and upon her return, Diane was nowhere to be seen. Her family knew she was off her meds, and they were very worried about her, but they also knew how unpredictable she was. She could have been literally anywhere.

Reports later surfaced that Diane was observed at a bar called the Hay Loft a few miles from Deborah's house. It seems unlikely that she would have walked all that way, so it's assumed that she either hailed a taxi or hitched a ride from someone. At any rate, once she got to the Hay Loft, she was the life of the party—that is, until she became so wild and unruly that the bartender refused to serve her any more drinks. When the flow of alcohol was finally cut off, she began "acting weird and walking in circles" talking to herself. She left the bar shortly thereafter, and the next anyone saw of her she was walking north on US 19. She ended up staying at the Coral Sands Motel, just off the same road and was seen having lunch there on April 14th.

Shortly thereafter, Diane's mother, Mildred Young, received a most unsettling message on her answering machine. When she got home and pressed the button to play it, she heard her daughter's voice on frantically shouting, "Help! Let me out!" As Mildred helplessly listened in, she then heard what sounded like a scuffle, followed by a man shouting, "Hey, gimme that!" before the phone was abruptly hung up. Mildred immediately tried to call back, but no one ever picked up.

Investigation

The next number Mildred dialed was that of her local police station. The cops tried to trace the call she'd received on her answering machine but were unsuccessful. The caller ID simply read "Starlight" and there was nothing more that could be gleaned from it.

The next day, April 15th, brought even more disturbing tidings in the form of a severed fingertip found off US 19—the very road that Diane had been seen walking along. The police crosschecked the fingertip with prints that had been taken when Diane had previously been arrested, and it was confirmed to be hers. What wasn't so clear was how it had become detached from her finger. Detectives couldn't tell whether it had been cut off deliberately, been severed during a fight, or perhaps even been slammed in a car door as a kidnapper forced Diane into his vehicle.

On April 18th, Deborah, who worked at a local convenience store, made a discovery of her own. A plastic bag that had been left in the store's freezer turned out to contain a set of Diane's clothes, neatly folded and stacked. However, there was no telling whether Diane herself had stashed the bag there before her disappearance or someone else had placed it there after the fact—and after that, there were no more developments in the case for over two years.

Intriguingly, the next lead, when it came, was the same as the last. On November 24, 2000, another plastic bag full of articles that belonged to Diane—makeup, this time—was found at the convenience store. Now it was obvious that someone was dropping off Diane's stuff after her disappearance—but whether it was Diane herself was still anyone's guess.

Update

Another major point of interest, in this case, occurred on June 27, 2001, when the Coral Sands Motel, where Diane had been staying just before she disappeared, was robbed. The place was owned by one Gary Robert Evers and his fiancée, Rose Kasper. Rose was in the office when masked gunmen forced their way inside, demanded money, and began to beat her viciously. Fortunately, Gary heard the commotion from a back room and came running out to face the intruders, gun in hand. The frightened thugs promptly turned tail and ran, and if Gary and Rose had simply reported the incident to the police, that probably would have been the end of it.

Instead, Gary decided to take the law into his own hands. He believed that one of the assailants was a 26-year-old named Todd Krammers who had been hanging around the motel, so the next day he invited Todd over to interrogate him. Todd denied involvement in the attempted robbery, but apparently, his word wasn't good enough for Gary, who then pulled out his gun and shot him dead.

Police would later determine that Todd was actually telling the truth and was not one of the would-be robbers. But it was too late for him, and too late for Gary, who was sent to prison for murder.

This incident gave rise to a new theory about what happened to Diane. Gary was obviously a violent man, and Diane was staying in Gary's motel the day she vanished. Could Gary have had something to do with her disappearance?

If he did, he never said anything before he eventually died in prison. And of course, the connection between him and Diane is fairly tangential and perhaps entirely coincidental. But some 20 years on, nobody has come up with any other answers as to what happened to Diane Augat. We can only hope that someday they will.

Ciara Breen
Where Have You Been?

Who: Ciara Breen
When: February 13, 1997
Where: Dublin, Ireland

Context

Her name is Ciara Breen, and hers has long been one of the most infamous missing person cases in all of the emerald isles of Ireland. Ciara vanished without a trace in February of 1997, just prior to her 18th birthday. Although most suspect she was the victim of foul play, the truth is that no one knows for sure.

On That Day

In the early morning hours of Thursday, February 13, 1997, Ciara's mother, Bernadette, checked on her teenage daughter—only to find her bed empty. Bernadette was alarmed, but she decided to hold off on alerting the authorities because she considered that perhaps Ciara had simply slipped outside to hang out with friends. She'd done it once a few years before, and Bernadette had called the police that time, but it turned out that

Ciara had just run off with one of her girlfriends and was perfectly safe. The two teenagers were squatting in an abandoned home on the other side of town, and after a few days, they got tired of their adventure and returned of their own accord.

So Bernadette didn't really begin to worry until after the sun had risen and there was still no sign of Ciara. Nevertheless, she had an important medical appointment at nine, and she accordingly left home and made her way to a clinic in Dublin. It was at this clinic that she received the devastating news, but it was nothing to do with her daughter—Bernadette had cancer and would need intensive rounds of chemo and radiation.

Investigation

When Bernadette returned to her house and Ciara still wasn't back, she finally decided to notify the Garda (the Irish police) that her daughter was missing. The police began canvassing the local area in search of Ciara Breen, and Bernadette Breen began praying that her daughter had simply run off again and would once again come back in a few days. Sadly, this time around, Ciara would not return after a few days or even a few months—this time, she was gone for good.

The investigation into her disappearance revealed that one of the last places Ciara was seen, was a local fast food joint. She'd been hanging out with some classmates, drinking soda and eating chips. The venue was a habitual gathering place for local teenagers, and in fact, they were often the only clientele. But on this particular day, the regulars would recall a stranger who was "twice their age" hanging around and interacting with them.

This was a man named Leo Flynn, and Ciara was already quite familiar with him—so familiar that Bernadette had explicitly told her to stay away from him. But the rebellious teenager was hardly going to let her mother's advice get in the way of having fun. According to the witnesses at the fast food restaurant, Ciara and Leo were acting quite chummy with each other. They heard him ask her if he could see her later that day—and they heard Ciara reply that she would sneak out after her mother went to bed.

Forensic evidence from the Breen house seemed to indicate that she'd followed through on that promise. There was no forced entry, just a window that had been opened from the inside. And the fingerprints present were those of Ciara, and Ciara alone. Investigators were fairly certain that she had climbed down from her window of her own accord between midnight and one in the morning. Furthermore, her friends confirmed that she had snuck out like this on several occasions unbeknownst to her mother.

The obvious question then was where Ciara had gone. Had she kept her rendezvous with Leo? And if so, was Leo behind her disappearance? However, the Garda couldn't even ask these questions at first. Leo refused to speak with them, and with no real evidence that any crime had been committed, it was not going to be easy to get a warrant for his arrest. Still, they kept pushing to bring Leo in on suspicion of murder, and on September 12, 1999, they finally got their warrant and took him into custody.

Detectives immediately began interrogating Leo about Ciara's disappearance, but if they were hoping for a confession, they were sorely disappointed. In fact, they were sorely disappointed if they were simply hoping for a halfway believable story. Instead of denying that he'd seen Ciara that night, or denying that he'd done anything to harm her, Leo actually denied knowing her in the first place! He doggedly stuck to this point even when the cops brought in one of the eyewitnesses who'd seen him hanging out with the girl. He just wouldn't budge.

Investigators knew somebody was lying, and between Leo and a half-dozen of Ciara's friends, their money was on Leo. Of course, that still didn't prove he'd killed her—and they couldn't find anything else that did, either, even after a very thorough search of his property. With no case against him, they had no choice but to let him go.

Update

Leo Flynn continued to live in the area for the next 20 years even while many whispered that he was responsible for Ciara's disappearance. In 2017 he was arrested for drunk driving and died of a "suspected overdose" while in police custody, apparently because he swallowed a bunch of illicit drugs just prior to being arrested in order to hide them. If he knew anything about what happened to Ciara, he took that knowledge with him to his grave.

Bernadette survived him by a year, ultimately succumbing to cancer in the summer of 2018 without ever finding out what actually befell her daughter. In fact, all anyone knows for sure is the same thing Bernadette knew on that fateful day in February of 1997: Ciara Breen climbed out of her window in the middle of the night—and disappeared without a trace.

Asha Degree Vanished Off the Face of the Earth

Who: Asha Degree
When: February 14, 2000
Where: Shelby, North Carolina

Context

Little Asha Degree was only nine years old when she disappeared in the spring of 2000. Her case has greatly perplexed investigators because there are some indications that she ran away from home, and others pointed to kidnapping—and yet neither of those explanations really makes sense. Asha had no apparent reason to run away, and her parents had gone to great lengths to ensure that she wouldn't be targeted by an abductor.

She came from a fairly happy home. Her mother and father were both hard workers and respected members of the community. Perhaps the only thing unusual about them was how protective they were of their daughter. Or, as her mother, Iquilla, would later admit, maybe a bit overprotective. They were careful who she was around, and they wouldn't allow her to have a computer for fear of strangers online. As Iquilla explained it, "Every time you turned on the TV there was some pedophile who had lured somebody's child away via the internet."

On That Day

On February 14, 2000, for reasons unknown to anyone but her, Asha woke up at three in the morning. She shared a bedroom with her 10-year-old brother, O'Bryant, but he barely registered it. He did recall hearing the bed squeak, but he thought she was just tossing and turning in her sleep. In fact, she was up, dressed, and reaching for a backpack full of clothing and supplies. For whatever reason, Asha was leaving, and she had prepared to do so well ahead of time.

It wasn't a pleasant day to run away from home if that's indeed what she was doing. The weather was cold, windy, and rainy, and several drivers noted the odd sight of the little girl walking by herself along North Carolina Highway 18 in the downpour. Dressed in a white long-sleeved T-shirt and white pants, she stood out easily in those early morning hours. At about 3:30, a trucker, thinking it "strange [that] such a small child would be out by herself at that hour," turned his rig around and tried to approach her to make sure she was alright. But when she realized she'd been spotted, she immediately turned and ran into some nearby woods.

Now, she could have fled from the truck driver for a couple of reasons. Maybe she was running away from home and didn't want to be caught, or maybe she was afraid that the trucker meant her harm—after all, her mother had always warned her not to talk to strangers. But once she made that fateful decision to head off into the trees, no one would see her ever again.

Investigation

When Asha's parents woke up on that sad Valentine's Day morning and realized that she was gone, they immediately called the police. A massive search was convened, with authorities and community members all canvassing the area. At one point, a helicopter with infrared heat-detecting equipment was even deployed. This aircraft should have been able to pick up anyone moving around on the ground, but it found no sign of Asha.

The next day candy wrappers were discovered strewn inside a shed belonging to a business by the highway where Asha had last been seen. Asha's Mickey Mouse hair bow and several other items that belonged to her were found there as

well. Had Asha been hiding out in the shed? And if so, where had she gone next?
Investigators didn't know, and they weren't going to find out. The exhaustive search continued for the next week, but no further sign of Asha was ever found.

Update

In August of 2001, Asha's backpack, complete with her name and phone number, was uncovered at a construction site by Highway 18, wrapped in plastic and buried under rubble. This was the last piece of physical evidence in the case, but it would later come to light that Asha had been planning to leave for some time, meticulously packing all the things that she would need. It also turned out that her fourth-grade class had recently studied a book called *The Whipping Boy*—which is about two kids who run away from home.

Asha was pretty young for a runaway, but many still believe that she was imitating the children in this book. In the story, though, the kids run away, have a merry old adventure, and then come back home. Sadly enough, in the case of Asha Degree, there has been no such homecoming.

Looking for Mathew Greene

Who: Mathew Greene
When: 2013
Where: Northern California

Context

Mathew Greene has been missing since July of 2013. He was a 39-year-old high school teacher and avid outdoorsmen, and at the time of his disappearance, he was doing what he liked to do best—wilderness hiking. Specifically, Mathew and a few friends were hiking the sprawling heights of the Sierra Nevada around Mammoth Lakes in Northern California. They were moving to another area of the mountain range when Mathew had car trouble and had to let his friends go on without him while he went into town to find a mechanic. Unfortunately, the local auto shop informed him that his vehicle had sustained a blown head gasket and would be in for a pretty intense overhaul.

On That Day

Mathew's phone records for the next few days show that he gave his parents a call and made a few calls to the shop where his car was being worked on. But by the time his friends came back to town on July 17th, he was nowhere to be seen. His car was there, all right, fully repaired and ready to drive, and most of his outdoor equipment was there too, but Mathew himself was gone. Also gone were his glacier-climbing gear and a few pages torn from a guidebook.

This was an important clue as to Mathew's whereabouts, as his friends knew that it was his habit to pull out the pages corresponding to the trail he wanted to hike. It seemed that Mathew had been contemplating a route that would take him through the sprawling Minerat area encompassing Mount Ritter and Mount Banner. But his name never appeared on any of the summit logs in the area—and Mathew himself never appeared again.

Investigation

Mathew Greene was officially reported missing on July 29, 2013. Police searched the campground where Mathew had left his car and the surrounding area, while Mathew's friends conducted their own unofficial search of not only the nearby wilderness trails but much of California in general. They spoke with people from all walks of life, posted fliers, and even chartered a private helicopter in an ultimately unsuccessful effort to find their missing friend.

To this day, no one knows where Mathew went—or just why he disappeared in the first place. Some have speculated that he got into an argument with the guys who repaired his car and subsequently stormed off. Maybe they overcharged him? But even if they did, stomping off into the wilderness without proper gear seems like a strange way to vent one's frustrations. Another theory is that Mathew was in a hurry to get away from someone else in Mammoth Lakes, but that just raises the question of who in that small town could have scared him so badly.

Others think that Mathew simply decided to taken an impromptu hike while waiting for his car to be fixed and, unprepared for it, died from the hazards of the environment he was trekking through. That does seem to be the most likely explanation, as Mathew had previously mentioned that he might try to "get on glacier ice," and the pages he took out of the guidebook covered the high, icy peak of Mount Ritter.

Update

There's still no sign of Mathew—or his remains—but in 2014, his distressed family went ahead and filed for a death certificate on the basis that he surely must have somehow lost his life in those high peaks near Mammoth Lakes. Did he? As of right now, he's still listed as missing, and no one really knows for sure.

Where's Jennifer Dulos?

Who: Jennifer Dulos
When: May 24, 2019
Where: New Canaan, Connecticut

Context

Jennifer Farber Dulos disappeared on May 24, 2019. Many contend that she was murdered—and indeed a murder case was initiated against her estranged husband. But since Jennifer's body has never been found, she is still very much a missing person.

On That Day

Jennifer kept a pretty tight schedule, and she vanished in the brief window of time between dropping her kids off at school and an appointment with her physician. She never arrived for that appointment, and after calls from a couple of her friends, police went to check on her home. They were in for a disturbing sight. Although there was no sign of Jennifer, they found a copious amount of her blood in the garage, along with indications that a struggle had taken place.

Investigation

It was pretty clear that Jennifer had been attacked and taken against her will. But by whom? Her husband, Fotis Dulos, was the natural suspect: The two were embroiled in a volatile divorce, and when they first separated in 2017, Jennifer had reported that Fotis was abusive and she was afraid of him.

Given these red flags, detectives would have been negligent not to give Fotis a long, hard look—but some have since complained that they zeroed in on him so completely that they closed their minds to any other possible suspects.

Convinced that Fotis was the culprit, they developed the theory that he had ambushed his wife, murdered her, and then "bundled her up with zip ties for transport to another location." Then he and his girlfriend, Michelle Troconis, disposed of the evidence in trash bags which they dumped around Hartford, Connecticut. On January 7, 2020, Fotis was arrested on charges of murder and kidnapping. Meanwhile, Michelle was charged with conspiracy to commit murder—and incredibly enough, so was Fotis's lawyer, Kent Douglas Mawhinney. Authorities seemed to believe that there was a whole cabal of plotters involved in Jennifer's disappearance and supposed death.

However, they still couldn't find her body, and Fotis steadfastly proclaimed his innocence throughout. Bailed out to the tune of six million dollars, he went back to his home in Farmington, Connecticut.

Three weeks later, on January 28th, he was found slumped in his car in his garage, incapacitated and fading fast. Having chosen to end his life by way of carbon monoxide poisoning, he had hooked a tube to the vehicle's exhaust pipe and placed the other end inside. He then sat with the car running until he succumbed to the fumes. He was rushed to the hospital, where he lingered for a couple of days before perishing on January 30th.

Had he killed himself out of remorse for murdering Jennifer? Well, not according to his suicide note, in which he continued to maintain that he had nothing to do with her disappearance. In fact, the note insisted that it was continued police harassment and his determination not to spend "one more hour" in prison for a crime that he "did not commit" that led him to take his own life. His family, at least, believed him, claiming that his arrest had been a "gross miscarriage of justice."

The police, meanwhile, with their main suspect dead, had no choice but to turn their attention to those on the periphery—Fotis's girlfriend Michelle Troconis and Fotis's attorney Kent Mawhinney.

But both still maintain their innocence, Jennifer is still missing, and no one is any closer to finding out what actually happened to her.

Update

On May 21, 2020, Michelle Troconis came forward to make a somewhat ambiguous statement. While maintaining her innocence in Jennifer's disappearance, she said that she had "made a mistake" in trusting Fotis Dulos. This, of course, could mean a wide variety of things, but it only adds to the shadow that continues to haunt Fotis even after his demise.

Oscar Zeta Acosta
The Brown Buffalo and his Boat of White Snow

Who: Oscar Zeta Acosta
When: 1974
Where: Mazatlan, Mexico

Context

Oscar Zeta Acosta was born to Juanita and Manuel Acosta in El Paso, Texas, in 1935. After high school, he served a brief stint in the Air Force before receiving a discharge in the 1960s. He then headed over to Modesto, California, to take classes at Modesto Junior College. From there he transferred to San Francisco State University, where he proved to be an excellent student, and after graduating he continued on to law school. He was admitted to the California Bar in 1966 and immediately began work for the Legal Aid Society in East Oakland, where he focused on representing disadvantaged and poor residents.

It was around this time that Oscar befriended the writer Hunter S. Thompson, who would later immortalize him by basing a character on him in the epic novel *Fear and Loathing in Los Vegas*. Meanwhile, Oscar was becoming an increasingly prominent fixture in the community. In 1970 he even ran for sheriff in Los Angeles County, although he lost by over a million votes. Oscar then went on to try his own hand at writing, publishing two semi-autobiographical works about his life and legal career. The title of the first, *Autobiography of a Brown Buffalo*, gave him the nickname that would be his calling card for the rest of his life.

On That Day

For such a high-profile figure, Oscar left remarkably little trace when he vanished in the summer of 1974. He was in Mazatlan, Mexico, at the time, although no one has any idea what he was doing there. The last anyone heard of him was when he called his son Marco to say that he was "about to board a boat full of white snow"—which could very well refer to a shipment of cocaine.

Investigation

For obvious reasons, many suspect that Oscar may have gotten mixed up with drug smugglers who killed him and either dumped his body at sea or left it somewhere in the sands of a remote Mexican desert. Oscar's former friend Hunter S.

Thompson, who conducted his own investigation into the mysterious disappearance, championed this view in a 1977 article for *Rolling Stone* entitled, in true gonzo style, "The Banshee Screams for Buffalo Meat."

Other theories range from an accidental overdose on that "white snow" to an assassination related to Oscar's political activism. But as notorious as Oscar Zeta Acosta used to be, if he's still alive, he's been keeping a very low profile since the 70s. There have been occasional claims of someone sighting him "in a bar" or "riding in a speedboat" somewhere, but these alleged fleeting glimpses of the brown buffalo have never been verified.

Update

In the fall of 2018, filmmaker Philip Rodriguez began work on a documentary about Oscar called *The Rise and Fall of the Brown Buffalo*. This film aims to not only to tell the story of Oscar's life but also to finally get to the bottom of his disappearance. We can only hope that this movie will generate some additional leads.

Gary Mathias and
The Yuba Five

Who: Gary Mathias
When: February 24, 1978
Where: Yuba, California

Context

One of the not only strange but outright confusing cases of mysterious disappearance occurred in 1978 in the Northern California town of Yuba City. Here a group of five young men ran headlong into a startling fate that left four of them dead in the wilderness—all of them, that is, except for Gary Mathias.

Ted Weiher, Bill Sterling, Jack Huett, Jack Madruga, and Gary Mathias were all in their early 20s to early 30s. They had met in a day program for adults with disabilities, and they all had various psychological conditions ranging from severe to minor. Gary, for example, suffered from schizophrenia. They came from different backgrounds, too, but they were unified by their love of sports, and their activities together usually revolved around this favorite pastime.

On That Day

On the night that the strange saga of the Yuba Five began, they watched a college basketball game at California State University, Chico. After the game, they were seen at a nearby convenience store buying a bunch of soda, snacks, and cartons of milk. Apparently, though, this wasn't just a pit stop for munchies—they were stocking up for an impromptu excursion into the mountainous wilderness outside of town.

Unfortunately, they had picked the worst possible time for such a jaunt. A rare blizzard was moving through this rough region of Northern California, all but paralyzing traffic, and indeed the group ended up getting stuck in a snowdrift.

Then, for some reason, they abandoned their car. It was a fateful decision, and seemingly an unnecessary one because it should have been easy enough for five healthy young men to push the vehicle back onto the road.

That was certainly the opinion of another motorist who was stranded in the snow that night. This older man *had* attempted to push his car out, by himself, and had suffered a mild heart attack for his trouble. Incapacitated, he got back in his car to wait for help. Then he saw a group of men approaching. They were carrying flashlights and seemed to be looking for something. Strangely, when he called out to them, they immediately switched off the lights and headed in the other direction.

If this group was Gary and his companions, as seems likely, why were they so quick to scurry off? Just what were they afraid of? Whatever the reason, they vanished into the night. That was the last time any of them were seen alive, and it wouldn't be until months later when the snow had melted, that four of the five would be found dead.

Investigation

On June 4, 1978, Ted Weiher's body was discovered inside a ranger's cabin. He and his companions had apparently broken into the cabin for shelter during the blizzard, but only his corpse was still there. Ted was skin and bones, with a full beard on his face, which seemed to indicate that he had been there for a while before he starved to death. Why he would have starved to death in a cabin that was fully stocked with canned food was anybody's guess.

Ted's body was wrapped up in a kind of shroud made from eight sheets, so it was clear that others were with him when he died. Where had they gone? Investigators started searching, and over the next few days, the corpses of Bill Sterling and

Jack Madruga were discovered several miles away. They were badly decomposed and it was evident that wild animals had begun feeding on them. Jack Huett was discovered next, his mortal remains reduced to little more than a skeleton. That accounted for four of the Yuba Five—but what about Gary Mathias?

Well, Gary has never been found, and this has led some to speculate that there was some sort of foul play involved and that Gary was behind it all. Despite his struggles with schizophrenia, Gary was highly intelligent and was regarded as a kind of ringleader for the group. More ominously, he was known to suffer from sudden breaks with reality that resulted in violent episodes. He had been discharged from the military for this very reason. It has also been alleged that he had attacked family members in the past.

Now, all of that might indicate that Gary could have killed his friends, or at least led them to their deaths—but if he was so unstable and erratic, could he really have stayed off the radar since then? Yet there hasn't been any sign of him whatsoever since the night of the basketball game and the blizzard way back in 1978.

The most logical explanation is probably that Gary died along with his friends, but his remains just haven't been found. Maybe he went for help and became lost in an even more remote area than where the rest of the men were recovered. Perhaps a bear or a mountain lion hauled off his body. It's a perfectly plausible scenario—but we just don't know if it's the truth.

And even if it is, it wouldn't answer the most perplexing question of all—why did the Yuba Five end up in the wilderness to begin with? Did they simply make a wrong turn? Or was there a reason that they went up into those mountain reaches? A relative of one of the men later remarked that he felt that something had "called them up there." What could it have been?

Update

This case has no further updates at this time, just many questions and few answers. We can only hope that someday some sort of closure will be achieved.

The Tragic Case of Diane Suzuki

Who: Diane Suzuki
When: July 6, 1985
Where: Aiea, Hawaii

Context

The disappearance of Diane Suzuki has baffled investigators for decades. She was a radiant 19-year-old dance instructor at the Rosalie Woodson Dance Academy in Aiea, Hawaii. Dance, and a young man named Lester Gantan, were the loves of Diane's life—a life that tragically came to an end when she disappeared in July of 1985. Ominously, her disappearance occurred during a spate of murders in which nine women were killed one after the other. While Diane's body has never been found, given the circumstances, no one is very hopeful that she's still alive somewhere.

On That Day

Diane Suzuki vanished without a trace on the afternoon of July 6, 1985. She and her girlfriends had been planning a weekend excursion to the beach, and after she got off work at the dance studio at 3:00 PM, Diane was supposed to drive directly to the rendezvous. But her car never left the parking lot.

What happened to Diane after she clocked out? One theory is that, that she was kidnapped while walking to her car. Another, even more, startling theory, is that she was killed inside the dance studio itself and her murder was somehow covered up. As of this writing, though, neither has been proven.

Investigation

The first real lead in the disappearance of Diane Suzuki came from her own parents, who were understandably concerned when her friends told them that she had failed to meet up with them. They immediately headed over to the dance studio to see if she might be working late. They were relieved to find her car in the parking lot—and then alarmed to find no sign of her. This being 1985, they couldn't exactly call up her cell phone, so they just parked nearby, hoping that she would return.

Sadly, she never did, but their stakeout did produce one clue that would later prove to be significant. Diane's parents saw several people leaving the dance studio carrying a large trunk of some sort. They maneuvered the big, bulky piece of luggage into a car, then piled inside themselves and drove off.

Could Diane—alive or dead—have been inside that trunk? That would provide an explanation as to how she inexplicably vanished that day. Was she carried out of the dance studio right under the noses of her coworkers, clients, and even her parents? It's a disturbing thought, but one that investigators decided should be considered.

Because right away, police were considering the worst-case scenario: that Diane wasn't only missing, but dead. They, therefore, sprayed her workplace with a substance called luminol, which has the ability to illuminate drops of blood that can't be seen with the naked eye. Even if a murderer wiped away the blood splatter, it would be revealed due to the chemical reaction of the luminol with the hemoglobin. And the cops' hunch was right. Blood was indeed discovered at the scene.

So, what about the people seen carrying the trunk out of the studio that day? Police identified them as one Dewey Hamasaki, his father, and his sister. Dewey worked at the studio with Diane and reportedly had quite a crush on her. Now, most cases of unrequited love don't lead to murder, of course, but Dewey was brought in for questioning all the same.

When he was, detectives noticed that he was suffering from several serious scratches. As such abrasions could be an indication of a struggle, they immediately became very keen to figure out what had caused them. Did Diane scratch Dewey while trying to get away from him? Dewey steadfastly denied this, insisting that he'd gotten the scratches from a rooster on his dad's farm.

The Hamasakis did have a large pig farm nearby, but rather than seeing this as an alibi for the scratches, investigators were suspicious that the sprawling farmland could have been used as a burial site for Diane's body. They searched the grounds thoroughly, and although they never found Diane's remains, they did find a pile of women's clothing buried under a tree stump—clothing that seemed awfully similar to that which Diane had been wearing.

In the end, though, this was not enough evidence to charge the Hamasakis with anything, and the investigation was eventually dropped. Even without a body, Diane's family finally accepted that she was deceased and held a funeral for her in 1997. Her mother passed away just a year later.

Update

In 2011, several sets of remains were unearthed at a popular park in Pearl City, Hawaii. It seemed that a serial killer had picked this place for his dumping ground, and it initially raised hopes for closure in the Diane Suzuki case. But as tantalizing of a lead as this was, it turned out that none of the remains belonged to Diane, and there is still no trace of her as of this writing.

In Search of Amy Bechtel

Who: Amy Bechtel
When: June 23, 1997
Where: Lander, Wyoming

Context

Amy Bechtel was 24 years old when she vanished without a trace. She and her husband Steve were both University of Wyoming grads with a great love for the outdoors, most especially the rugged terrain of Wyoming. They were also fitness fanatics, and Amy herself was an Olympic marathon hopeful.

On That Day

On July 24, 1997, the day she disappeared, Amy Bechtel was teaching a course at the Wind Witness Fitness Center. She had told Steve that she was going to run a few errands after work, so he didn't expect her to come home until late in the day—but unfortunately, she never came home at all.

She was last seen at around 2:30 PM in the Camera Connection, a nearby photoshop. It is believed that she then drove to the Shoshone National Forest.

Investigation

On the afternoon that Amy disappeared, Steve came home around 4:30 PM after doing some rock climbing with a few friends. He wasn't surprised that Amy wasn't back yet, but after the sun went down and he still hadn't heard from her, he began to worry. He called up some family members and neighbors to join him in an unofficial search for his missing wife, and he also called the police to report her disappearance. Police search teams began scouring the area in the early morning hours of July 25th.

They didn't find Amy, but they did find her vehicle abandoned on the side of a dirt road at Shoshone National Forest. Amy's keys were inside, yet she was nowhere to be seen. The forest was well known for its bears and mountain lions, so the first thought was that Amy had fallen prey to one of these natural predators. But it wasn't long before investigators shifted gears to focus on predators of a more human kind. And in particular, they began to suspect Amy's own husband.

This was largely due to what they discovered in Steve's personal journals when they searched the Bechtel home. He wrote about feeling "violence toward women," and even more disturbingly, in some passages he highlighted the violence that he felt toward Amy in particular.

The police felt certain that this was their smoking gun in the case, so they decided to pull out one of the oldest tricks in the book to get Steve to confess. They brought him in for questioning and claimed that they had evidence proving he had murdered his wife. In reality, they had no evidence at all, but they lied through their teeth hoping to make Steve nervous enough to admit his guilt. This method has been used in quite a few cases, and in many of them (rightly or wrongly), it has worked.

Well, it didn't work on Steve. As soon as the interrogators started their shtick, Steve immediately ended the discussion and stopped cooperating with the authorities who he now realized were not so much out to find his missing wife—as they were out to get him.

It turns out that Steve had a good excuse for the contents of the journals that police had found so incriminating—they were lyrics he had written for the rock band he played in. And of course, any number of artists writing in dramatic terms about their romantic relationships could be misinterpreted as plotting literal violence. If the cops were to look at any given Nine Inch Nails song, for example, they might conclude that Trent Reznor has a penchant for homicide and several other felonies. Heck, even a couple Alanis Morrissette songs might be disturbing. Just because someone expresses themselves in dramatic terms in music does not make them a murderer.

At any rate, from the point forward Steve was very cautious about his interactions with police. He made sure to emphasize his alibi, pointing out that he was rock climbing with several friends at the time of Amy's disappearance. Those friends all backed him up, but that still wasn't good enough for the police, who then suggested that Steve take a lie detector test. However, he steadfastly refused. Maybe he was afraid of what the results might reveal—or maybe he was simply afraid of how the investigators, who had already indicated that they were trying to set him up to take the fall, would interpret the results. It should also be noted that Steve's lawyer, Kent Spence, counseled him not to agree to the test.

Instead of talking to the police, Steve began talking to just about everyone else in an effort to find his missing wife. He created a grassroots campaign to search for her that included the "Amy Wroe Bechtel Recovery Headquarters" (featuring Amy's likeness on the then-nascent World Wide Web) as well as other multimedia outlets. If Steve was a killer, he was a diabolically devious one.

When neither Steve nor the local cops turned up any sign of Amy by August, the FBI got involved. The G-men reviewed NASA satellite imagery of the area, but the pictures revealed very little. Follow-up shots in 1998 from the Russian space station Mir, were not of much help either.

Update

This case received a brief bump in 2003 when a hiker who was walking near where Amy disappeared discovered a Timex Iron Man digital watch just like the one Amy had been wearing prior to her disappearance. But it simply could not be determined whether or not the watch was Amy's, and as of right now, this case of mysterious disappearance remains wide open.

How Elijah Disappeared in the Blink of an Eye

Who: Prophet Elijah
When: 9th Century BC
Where: Israel

Context

The mysterious disappearance of the biblical prophet Elijah just might be the oldest one on record. Now, for those who take their Scripture literally, there is no mystery as to where Elijah went—he was snatched up by a whirlwind and taken to heaven. For the more skeptical-minded, though, that's just a fancy way of saying that he disappeared into thin air.

On That Day

Elijah was on a journey with his protégé Elisha. They were walking from the town of Gilgal to the town of Bethel in the north of Israel. But their journey was interrupted by a strange sighting in the sky and then a sudden conveyance of Elijah into the air. Or as the Old Testament tells us in 2 Kings 2:11, "And it came to pass, as they still went on, and talked, that, behold, there appeared a chariot of fire, and horses of fire, and parted them both asunder, and Elijah went up by a whirlwind into heaven."

Investigation

If what actually happened was anything like what the Bible describes, this was a very strange event indeed. But it wasn't the only reported event of its kind, and that fact inspired the ancient astronaut theorist Erich Von Daniken to write his famous book *Chariots of the Gods* in which he argues that such odd instances probably show the ancients struggling to describe advanced technology with the limited understanding available to them at the time.

The theory goes that if ancient people saw a spacecraft hovering above the ground, illuminating the darkness with bright flashing lights, they would likely have said that it was "on fire." They had no concept of artificial lighting; for them, the only thing that produced very bright light was fire. And since the only swift vehicles they knew were chariots, it's easy to see how an illuminated aircraft would become a "chariot of fire."

And what about the whirlwind? Well, it could just be that the "whirlwind" was a "wormhole" caused by a spacecraft with the ability to warp the fabric of space and time that then disappeared through the breach it had created.

Of course, three thousand years later, that's all just speculation. But whatever may have occurred, Elijah was never seen or heard from again. And it's not that no one looked for him—it's said that some 50 people canvased the area to see if perhaps the famous prophet could be found, but all of their efforts came to naught.

Update

Updates in this case depend on who you talk to. The Jews and Muslims will tell you there aren't any. Islam holds that Elijah won't be back until the end of the world, while in the Jewish tradition it is said that he will return to herald the coming of the Messiah. Christians, however, contend that he already did just that during the transfiguration of Jesus. Mormons, on the other hand, insist that Elijah made a cameo appearance to Joseph Smith on April 3, 1836. At any rate, Elijah's disappearance has proven to be a very memorable one, and many people are still looking for him to this very day.

Finding Them

Since the beginning of recorded human history, there have been stories of mysterious disappearances. The potential causes of these disappearances are many, but the repercussions are typically the same. Because for every soul that disappears, loved ones are left behind to pick up the pieces.

They say that in many ways, living with the uncertainty of a missing loved one is worse than dealing with their death. One is forever stuck in a limbo world of uncertainty about what actually transpired. You don't know if the missing person is alive or dead, yet the grief is just as bad as if they had died right in front of you.

Those who have lost loved ones in this manner are cheated of even the closure that a funeral could provide. Instead, they are simply left to wonder and second guess themselves for the rest of their years. The ways in which individuals vanish are many, but the burning desire of those who knew them is always the same.

What they want more than anything else is to tie up the void that has been torn into their lives by the terrible tragedy of the ever-present loss they face. All they want to do is put the sadness and worry behind them. All they so desperately want to do—is find them.

Further Readings

As we bring this book to a close, I wanted to take the time to share with you some of the reference and reading materials that were part of my research. If you would like to learn more about any of the stories presented here, please feel free to examine any or all of these resources and references in full.

Hard-Boiled Hollywood: Crime and Punishment in Postwar Los Angeles. Jon Lewis In this book, Mr. Lewis explains just how interconnected Hollywood was with the criminal world in Los Angeles. Of particular interest for this book was his take on the disappearance of Jean Spangler.

Top Secret Alien Abduction Files: What the Government Doesn't Want You to Know. Nick Redfern It's always a refreshing jump down the rabbit hole with Nick Redfern and this book doesn't disappoint. He takes us on a journey through some of the strangest cases of paranormal activity; including an overview of a couple of the mysterious disappearances presented in this book.

Mysterious Disappearances in History. Enzo George Just as the name might imply, this book focusses on some of the strangest disappearances in history. This text was rather insightful for a wide variety of cases presented here.

Honolulu Homicide. Gary A. Dias and Robbie Dingeman. In the 48 contiguous states of America there is often a disconnect between Alaska and Hawaii. This book by Gary A Dias however, makes sure that tremendous insight is brought to the fore concerning the latter. This text is particularly helpful as it pertains to homicide and mysterious disappearances in Hawaii.

www.ingramcontent.com/pod-product-compliance
Ingram Content Group UK Ltd.
Pitfield, Milton Keynes, MK11 3LW, UK
UKHW040751200825
7485UKWH00011B/107